Easy Olympic Sports Readers

Track & Field

© 2004 by GRIFFIN PUBLISHING GROUP/United States Olympic Committee

Published by Griffin Publishing Group under license from the United States Olympic Committee. The use of the Olympic-related marks and terminology is authorized by the United States Olympic Committee pursuant to Title 36 *U.S. Code*, Section 220506. United States Olympic Committee, One Olympic Plaza, Colorado Springs, CO 80909.

All rights reserved. No portion of this book may be reproduced in any form without written permission of Griffin Publishing Group and Teacher Created Materials.

10 9 8 7 6 5 4 3 2 1

ISBN   1-58000-115-7
TCM   6138

DIR./OPERATIONS . . . . .Robin L. Howland
PROJECT MANAGER . . . . .Bryan K. Howland
AUTHOR .Eric Migliaccio
EDITOR . . . . .Ina Massler Levin, M.A.
DESIGNER . . . . .Phil Garcia
PHOTOGRAPHS . . . . .Getty Images
COVER PHOTOS . . . .(*top*) Mike Powell, Mike Powell
                                       (*bottom*) Ezra Shaw, Mike Powell

Published in association with
and distributed by:
Teacher Created Materials
6421 Industry Way
Westminster, CA 92683
www.teachercreated.com

Griffin Publishing Group
18022 Cowan, Suite 202
Irvine, CA 92614
www.griffinpublishing.com

Manufactured in the United States of America

Track and field is an Olympic sport.

Track and field athletes run, jump, or throw.

Sprinters run very fast for short distances.

The marathon is a very long race.

There are team relay races, too.

One runner passes a baton to his teammate.

Some athletes run and jump over hurdles.

Some use a pole to vault over a high bar.

Some jump as far as they can.

ANDY LYONS

Some jump as high as they can.

Some throw a metal ball called a **shot put** as far as they can.

MIKE POWELL

Some throw a metal plate called a **discus** as far as they can.

Some throw a spear called a **javelin** as far as they can.

There are 24 track and field events in all.

MIKE POWELL

That's 24 gold medals up for grabs!